THE REVOLUTION HANDBOOK

wren & rook

For Nanny Pat and Maia

First published in Great Britain in 2018 by Wren & Rook
Copyright © Hodder & Stoughton Ltd, 2018
All rights reserved.
ISBN: 978 1 5263 6122 6
10 9 8 7 6 5 4 3 2 1

Wren & Rook
An imprint of Hachette Children's Group
Part of Hodder & Stoughton
Carmelite House
50 Victoria Embankment
London EC4Y 0DZ
An Hachette UK Company
www.hachette.co.uk
www.hachettechildrens.co.uk

Printed in England

Publishing Director: Debbie Foy
Commissioning Editor: Liza Miller
Art Director: Laura Hambleton

Designed by Claire Yeo

THE REVOLUTION HANDBOOK

ALICE SKINNER

A BIT ABOUT ME AND THIS BOOK

My Instagram page started as a way for me to show the world how annoyed, frustrated and straight-up pissed off I am by it. I had no idea how much it would grow and that there would be so many people who shared my outrage. I believe that NOW is the time for us to stand up, protest and disrupt. I created *The Revolution Handbook* to help you record your thoughts and prepare to speak up – because sometimes there's nothing more scary than finding your voice. Use the book to explore your emotions and opinions, and to help you look after you, too.

There are no rules for completing it – dip in whenever you feel like it, or if you fancy a binge, tackle it all in one go. Pick up this book whenever you're feeling angry or frustrated at the world, and let it be a place for you to gather your thoughts and reflect. Then, put everything you've learned from it into action, and go STICK IT TO THE MAN.

All you need is a pen and some passion!

PS Use #therevolutionhandbook to share your ideas so we can all help cheer each other on.

WOULD YOU RATHER ...?

TEA
WITH
TRUMP?

KALE WITH
KIM
JONG-UN?

PIZZA
WITH
PUTIN?

1

2

5 THINGS YOU WANT TO SEE CHANGED AROUND THE WORLD

3

4

5

THAT'S TOO MANY!
PICK 3 TO TACKLE.

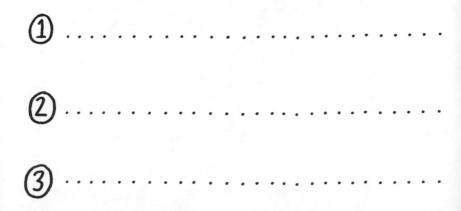

① . . . .

② . . . .

③ . . . .

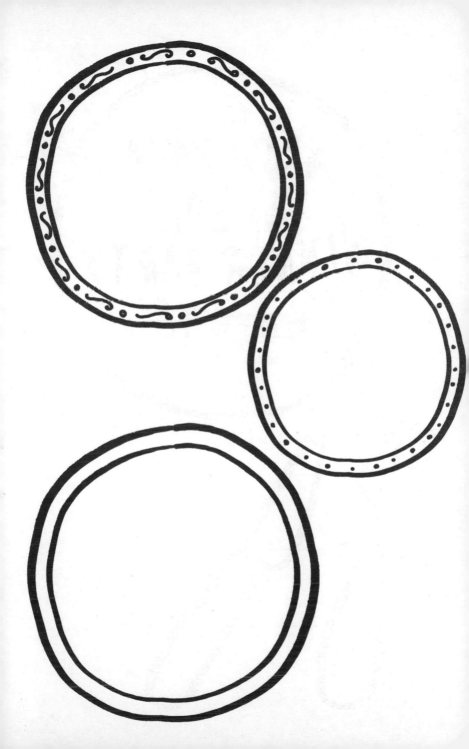

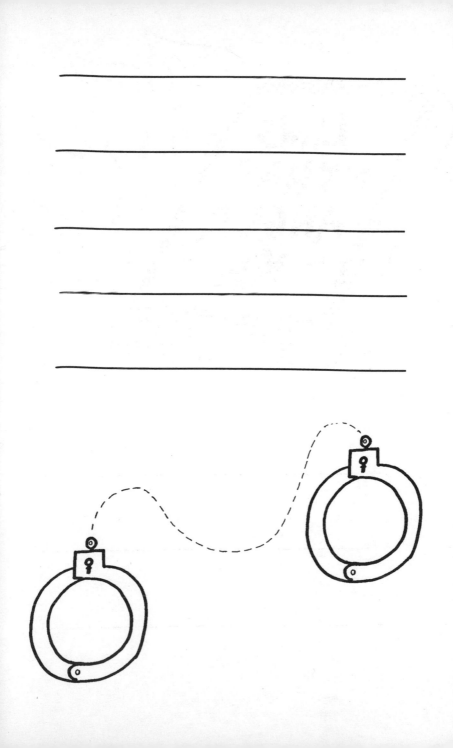

NEGATIVE THOUGHTS I HAVE

① ....

② ....

③ ....

HOW I CAN COMBAT THEM

REFLECTIONS FROM A MARCH

YOUR NEXT STEPS

. . . .

. . . .

. . . .

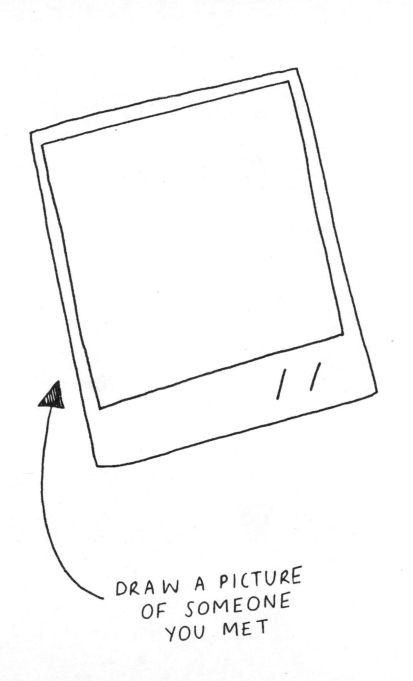

DRAW A PICTURE
OF SOMEONE
YOU MET

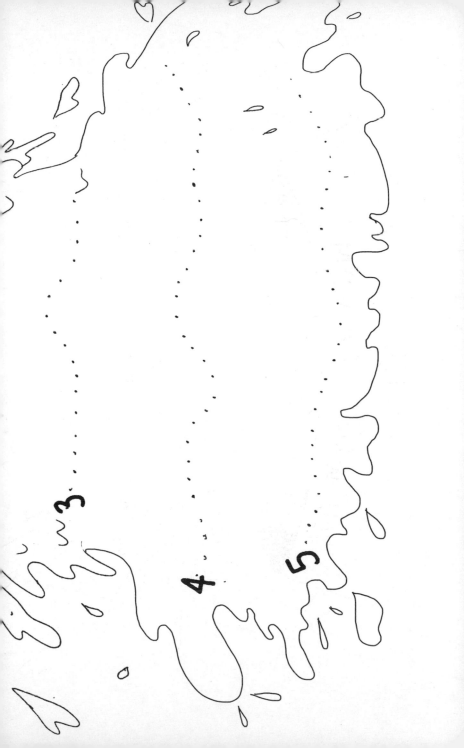

DESIGN A T-SHIRT slogan

THERE'S A SPECIAL
PLACE IN
HELL
FOR...

TOP 5 CAMPAIGNS THAT inspire ME

MY campaign HASHTAGS

\#

     \#

\#

     \#

\#

     \#

\#

WHO DO YOU NEED TO TARGET TO ACHIEVE YOUR GOALS?

BLACK LIVES MATTER

HOW YOU CAN SUPPORT BLM

- FIND OR CREATE BLM GROUPS
- GET INVOLVED AND GET ACTIVE, GO TO RALLIES AND MEETINGS
- USE THE HASHTAG ON SOCIAL MEDIA SPEAK UP AND SHARE IMPORTANT CONTENT

LIST THE WAYS THAT
ALL LIVES MATTER
IS OFFENSIVE CRAP:

. . . .

. . . .

. . . .

. . . .

. . . .

. . . .

SHUT DOWN

TWITTER COMEBACKS

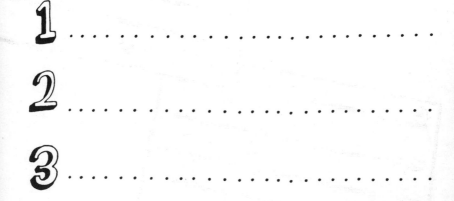

1 ....

2 ....

3 ....

TODAY
I'M
PISSED OFF
ABOUT

. . . .

. . . .

. . . .

STICK IN A PHOTO
OF YOURSELF
MAKING A DIFFERENCE

POST IT ON
INSTAGRAM
#THEREVOLUTIONHANDBOOK

Awesome strengths

THE STRENGTHS THAT YOU BRING TO A CAMPAIGN:

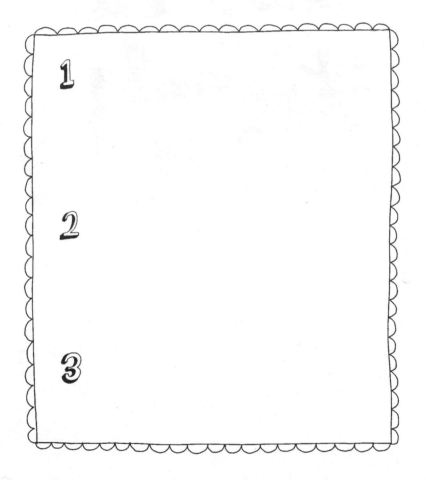

1

2

3

Stick in the DUMBEST headline from this week

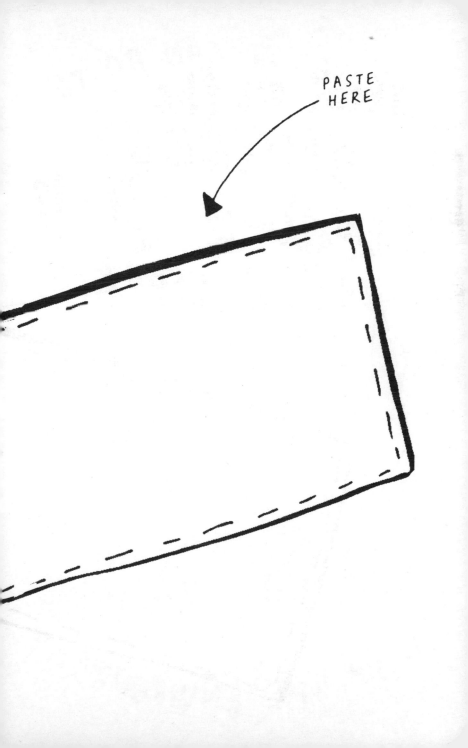

PASTE
HERE

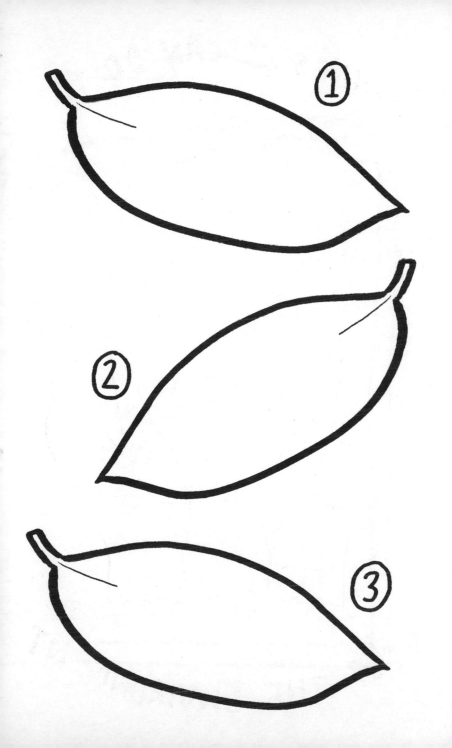

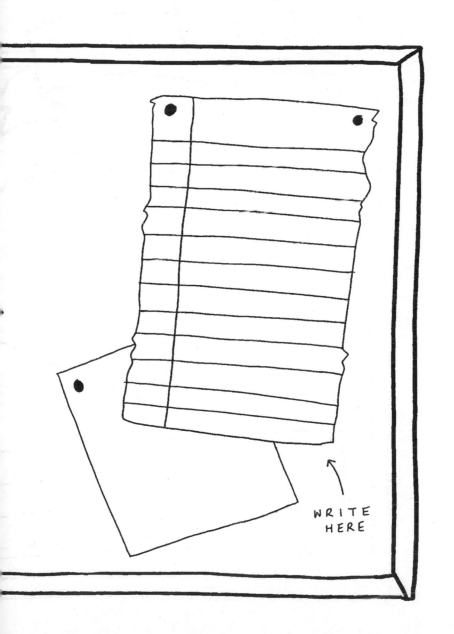

WRITE
HERE

READ A NEWSPAPER YOU WOULD NEVER NORMALLY PICK UP. LIST THREE THINGS THAT SURPRISE YOU.

TWEET YOUR
POLITICAL MESSAGE
IN 280 CHARACTERS

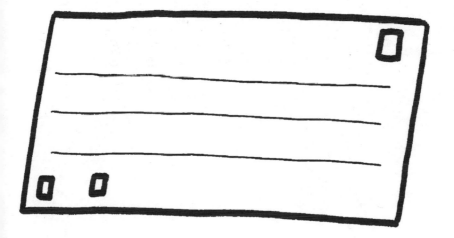

THE REVOLUTIONHANDBOOK

I WANT TO BE AN ALLY TO...

DRAW THEM

LIST THE REASONS WHY

1 . . . .

. . . .

. . . .

2 . . . .

. . . .

. . . .

3 . . . .

. . . .

. . . .

write a speech

ABOUT SOMETHING THAT MATTERS

protest PLANNING

CHECKLIST

- [ ] PLACARD
- [ ] GLOVES
- [ ] CAMERA
- [ ] MONEY
- [ ] WATER
- [ ] PEN AND PAPER

ENERGY

WATER

$5 $5

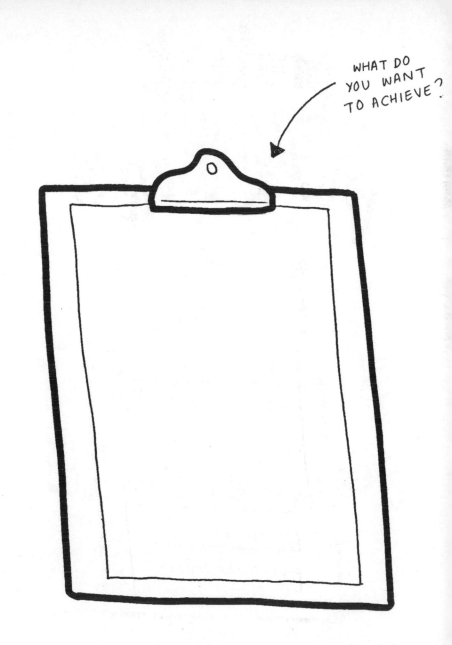

3 THINGS YOU LOVE ABOUT SOMEONE YOU ADMIRE

1 ....

2 ....

3 ....

HOW COULD THEY KICKSTART YOUR CAMPAIGN?

....

....

....

STICK IN
ACTIVISM
STICKERS
YOU'VE
COLLECTED

HOW ARE YOU

FEELING TODAY?

MARK IT ON THE LINE. YOU CAN ALWAYS COME
BACK AND REFER TO THIS PAGE.

IF I WERE IN CHARGE

OF THE COUNTRY
I WOULD:

WRITE HERE

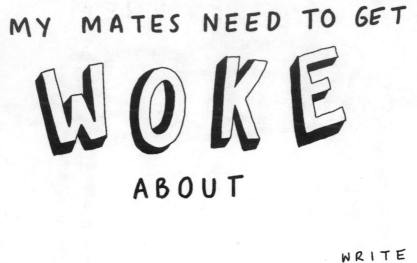

MY MATES NEED TO GET

WOKE

ABOUT

WRITE HERE

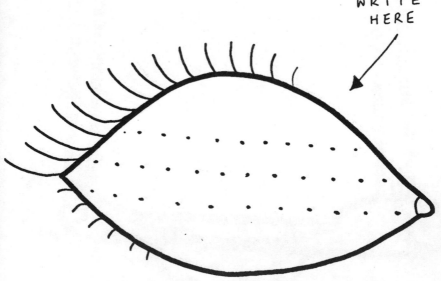

I'LL GET THEM

WOKE

BY

a guide to

INTERSECTIONALITY

THE INTERCONNECTED NATURE OF SOCIAL CATEGORIZATIONS SUCH AS RACE, CLASS & GENDER, REGARDED AS CREATING OVERLAPPING & INDEPENDENT SYSTEMS OF DISCRIMINATION OR DISADVANTAGE

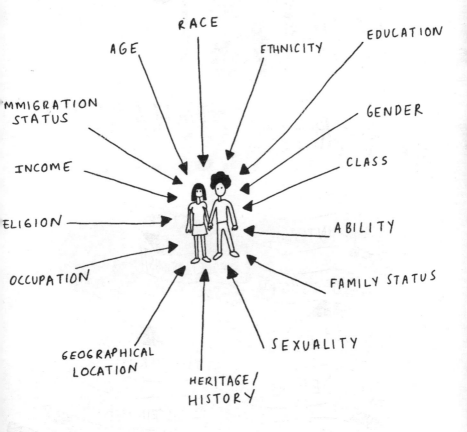

PROTEST MARCH

BABY WITH PROTEST SIGN	CELEB PROTESTOR	SOMEONE WEARING SOMETHING ANTI-TRUMP
SOMEONE IN FANCY DRESS	AN INSTAGRAM ACTIVIST	DOG WITH A SIGN
A POLICE PERSON WITH A SIGN	SOMEONE WITH THE SAME SIGN AS YOU	A TV REPORTER

name 3
songs
that
bring
about
political
change

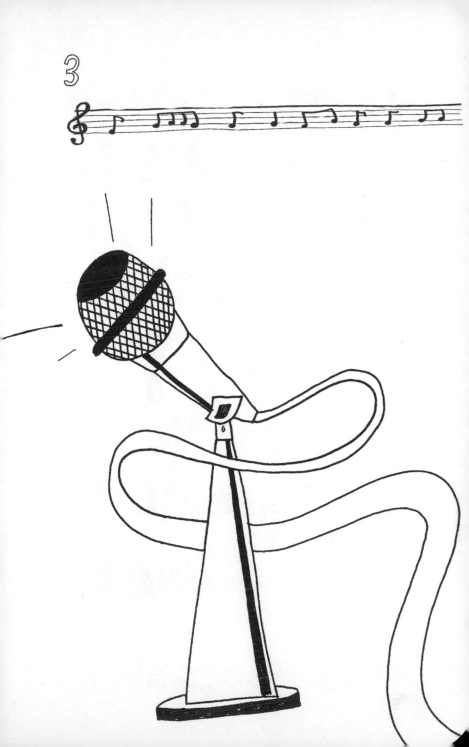

REST
advice

MEET UP WITH YOUR FRIENDS

TURN OFF YOUR PHONE

HAVE A LAUGH!

design your own political party

NAME:

LOGO:

SLOGAN:

THINGS THAT ARE ON YOUR MIND

THE GOOD

the FRIEND WHO INSPIRES you every day

WHO ARE THEY?

HOW DO THEY INSPIRE YOU?

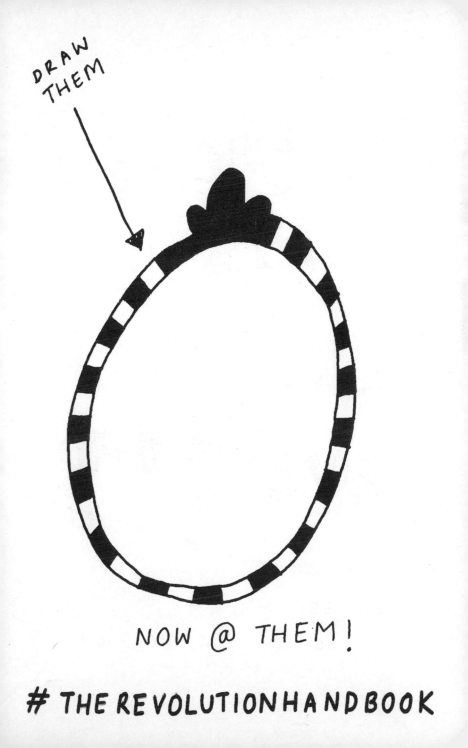

pictures
of you
and your
friends
at a
march

STICK IN

YOUR FAVOURITE
SPEECHES THAT HAVE CHANGED THE WORLD

DRAW A PIC OF YOUR HAPPY PLACE

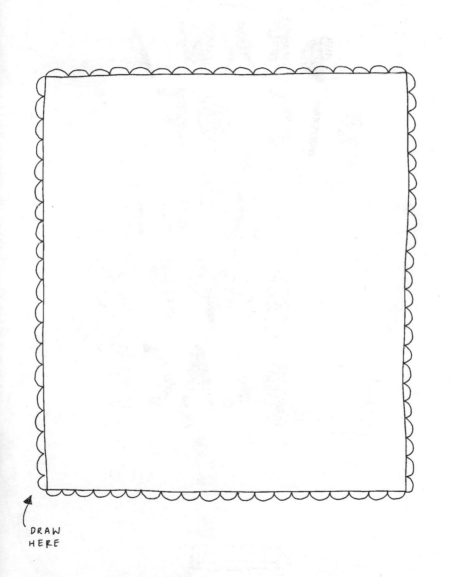

DRAW
HERE

FAVOURITE POLITICAL GAFFES

RECREATE THEM

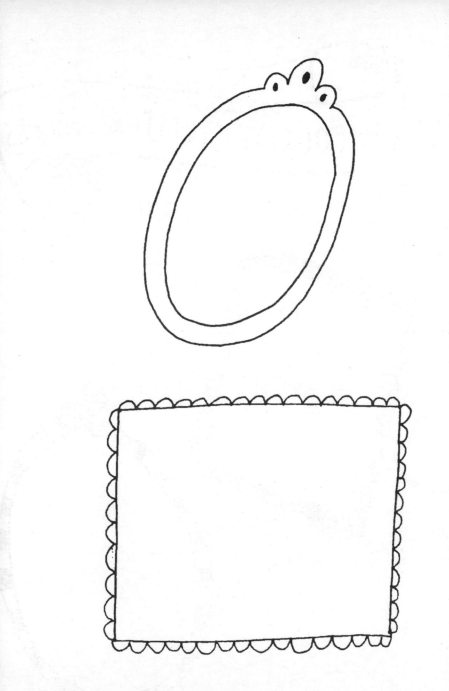

HASHTAGS THAT HAVE BEEN USED IN POLITICAL MOVEMENTS

\#

\#

\#

\#

design your placard

RECREATE SOME OF THE BEST SIGNS YOU'VE SEEN

DATE :

CHECK BACK
IN 365 DAYS AND COMPARE
WHERE YOU ARE!

WHAT WAS THE LAST HEADLINE THAT MADE YOU FREAK OUT?

WRITE
HERE

your

POLITICAL

BAE

STICK
IN A PIC
OF YOUR
ACTIVISM
HERO

CONFESSION TIME

3 TIMES YOU'VE REPOSTED SOMETHING FAKE BY ACCIDENT:

① . . . .

② . . . .

③ . . . .

PROTEST CHANTS YOU KNOW

CREATE YOUR OWN

- - - - - - - - - - - - - - - - - -

- - - - - - - - - - - - - - - - - -

- - - - - - - - - - - - - - - - - -

- - - - - - - - - - - - - - - - - -

- - - - - - - - - - - - - - - - - -

- - - - - - - - - - - - - - - - - -

YOUR FIRST

WHAT WAS THE FIRST TIME YOU EVER FOUND SOMETHING REALLY UNFAIR?

WRITE YOUR TOP 3 THINGS TO DO

WHEN THE WORLD GETS YOU DOWN

1 . . . .

2 . . . .

3 . . . .

FINIS...

TASKS YOU'VE STARTED BUT NEVER FINISHED

TICK THEM OFF WHEN
YOU'VE COMPLETED THEM

DREAM
headline

WHAT NEWSPAPER HEADLINE
WOULD YOU LOVE TO WAKE UP TO ?

WRITE
HERE

REBELS FROM HISTORY I ADMIRE

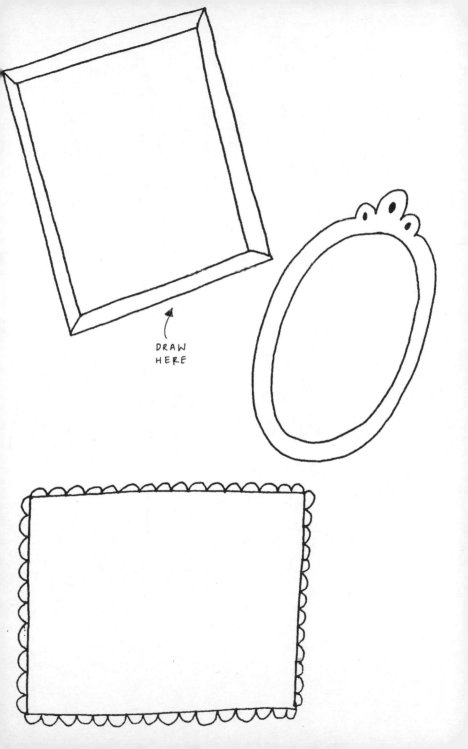

DRAW
HERE

RAGE!

CLOSE YOUR EYES
SCREAM,
SCRIBBLE ALL OVER THESE PAGES!

FEEL ANY BETTER?

MY FAVOURITE
INSPIRATIONAL
QUOTES

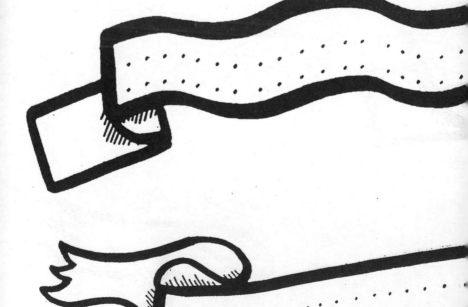

WRITE
HERE

DRAW THE BEST THING
THAT COULD POP UP ON
YOUR PHONE

...AND THE WORST

GRAFFITI on

CHECK *your* PRIVILEGE

LIST THE WAYS IN WHICH YOU'VE HAD ADVANTAGES IN LIFE.

TOP FILMS ABOUT ACTIVISM

1

2

3

MY SPIRIT COUNTRY

DRAW A POSTCARD FROM ITS CAPITAL CITY

which country's
policies do you
agree with
most?

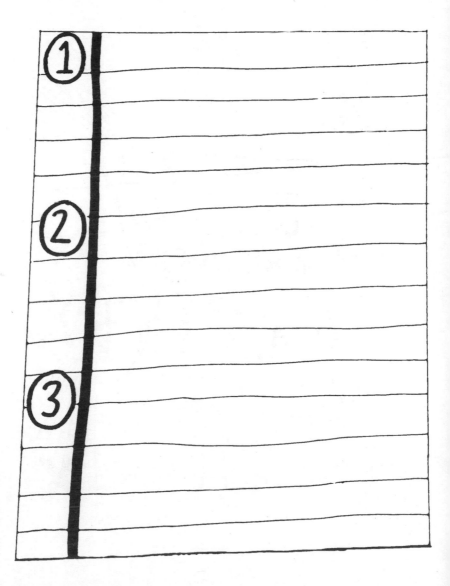

WHAT ARE THE THINGS
THAT STRESS YOU
OUT ON
SOCIAL MEDIA?

WHICH POLITICAL EMOJI IS YOUR PHONE CRYING OUT FOR?

DRAW
HERE

WHAT ARE THE
GENDER ISSUES
THAT DEPRESS
YOU MOST?

GOOD NEWS

NEWS STORIES THAT MAKE YOU HAPPY

ARE YOU DOING ALL YOU
CAN TO BE POLITICALLY
ENGAGED?

A YES I'M TRYING MY ABSOLUTE BEST
B TRYING HARD BUT COULD BE DOING MORE
C I'M DOING OK
D IF I'M HONEST, I'M SLACKING

IF YOU DIDN'T CHOOSE A,
WHAT ARE YOU GOING TO
DO ABOUT IT?

_____
_____
_____
_____
_____

ACTS OF DISOBEDIENCE

Log here the times you've stood up to an oppressor, disrupted the normal or questioned authority

☐ ....

....

☐ ....

....

☐ ....

....

THE REVOLUTIONHANDBOOK

THE REVOLUTIONHANDBOOK

THE REVOLUTIONHANDBOOK

THE REVOLUTIONHANDBOOK

THE REVOLUTIONHANDBOOK

THE REVOLUTIONHANDBOOK

3 TIMES YOU STUCK IT TO THE MAN

How to fight
islamophobia

- FIGHT IT BY INCREASING YOUR UNDERSTANDING OF ISLAM
- NAME IT AND CALL IT OUT FOR WHAT IT IS
- REPORT IT IF YOU SEE IT, WHETHER THAT BE ONLINE OR IN REAL LIFE
- BE AN ALLY IN ANY WAY YOU CAN
- SPEAK OUT IF IT HAPPENS AROUND YOU
- AVOID NEWS, MOVIES AND BOOKS THAT PROPAGATE IT

DRAW
SMASHES

SMASH
THE
glass ceiling

THREE WAYS YOU CAN HELP DISMANTLE THE PATRIARCHY

1 . . . .

2 . . . .

3 . . . .

"I contain

WHAT PEOPLE ASSUME WHEN THEY SEE ME

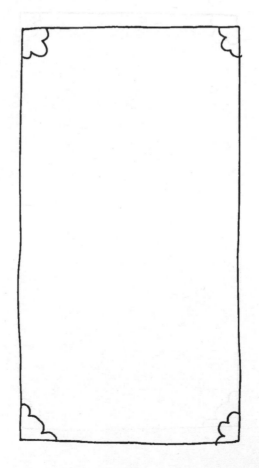

multitudes ")")

– WALT WHITMAN

WHO I REALLY AM

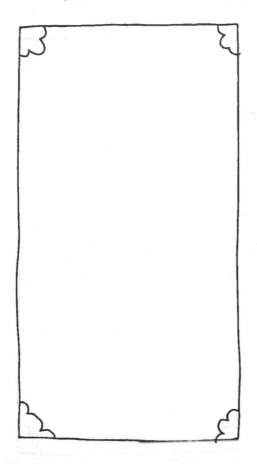

CHANGES YOU CAN MAKE

locally

SIGNATURES AND NOTES FROM FELLOW ACTIVISTS

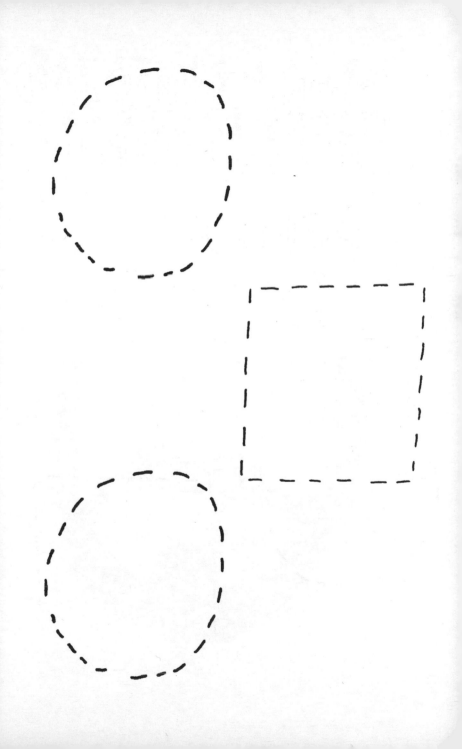

DRAW A POLITICIAN AROUND THE FUZZ

FAMOUS GAME CHANGERS

DRAW
HERE

LOG THEM HERE SO
YOU DON'T FORGET

HERO

OF THE WEEK

Election
debate

BINGO

DEBATE INTERRUPTED BY PROTESTOR	RAISED VOICES	SOMEONE CONTRADICTS THEMSELVES
FEMALE CANDIDATE INTERRUPTED	COMPLAINTS ABOUT THE MEDIA	REPETITIVE USE OF SOUNDBITES
POLITICIAN AVOIDING ANSWERING QUESTION	HISTORICAL QUOTE USED	HECKLED BY AUDIENCE

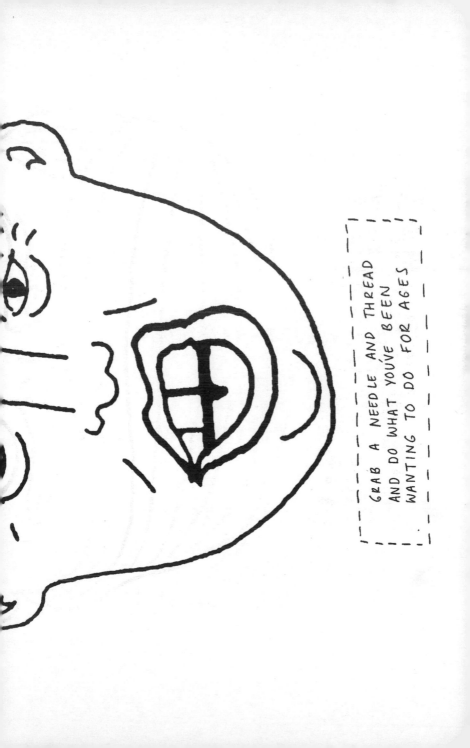

GRAB A NEEDLE AND THREAD
AND DO WHAT YOU'VE BEEN
WANTING TO DO FOR AGES

THE REVOLUTIONHANDBOOK

THE REVOLUTIONHANDBOOK

THE REVOLUTIONHANDBOOK

THE REVOLUTIONHANDBOOK

THE REVOLUTIONHANDBOOK

THE REVOLUTIONHANDBOOK

write a protest poem

MY BUCKET LIST

THINGS I WILL HAVE CHANGED
BEFORE I DIE

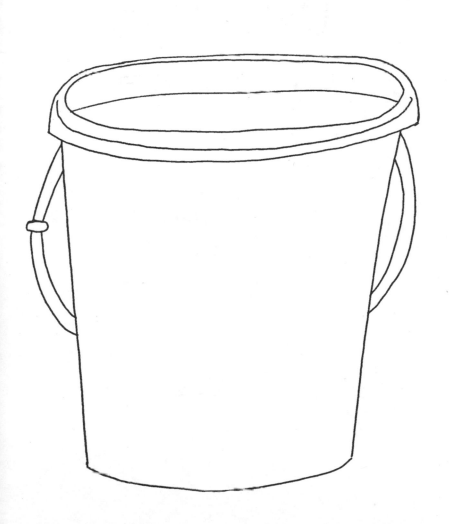

CAESAR

STALIN

BRING YOUR CAMPAIGN TO LIFE

THREE REAL PEOPLE WHO YOUR CAMPAIGN IS TRYING TO HELP

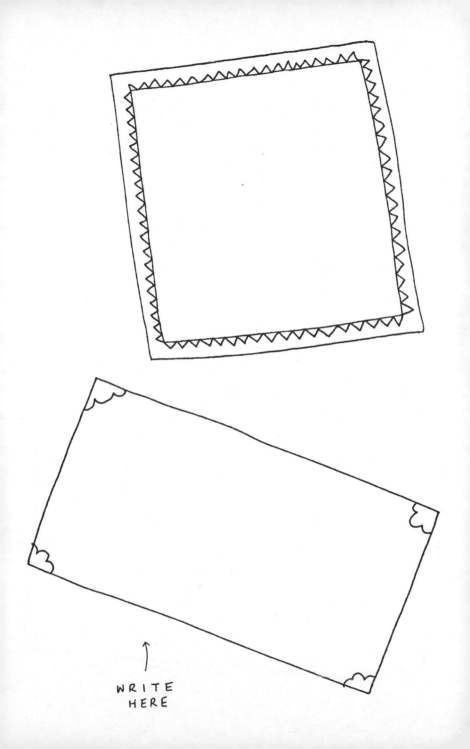

WRITE
HERE

YOUR PROUDEST MOMENT

DESCRIBE THE TIME YOU FELT MOST PROUD ABOUT SOMETHING YOU ACHIEVED AGAINST THE ODDS.

DEBATE PREP

PREP

YOUR MAIN ARGUMENTS

. . . .

. . . .

. . . .

CRITICISM YOU'LL RECEIVE

. . . .

. . . .

. . . .

YOUR COMEBACKS

. . . .

. . . .

. . . .

DRAW YOUR DREAM FUTURE

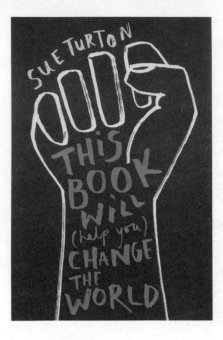

Paperback
September 2017
978 1 5263 6090 8

This Book Will (Help You)
Change the World
by Sue Turton

A practical and inspiring guide to activism and
politics, this book is a rallying call: if you don't like
the world you see in front of you, you have the
power to change it. Award-winning journalist Sue
Turton explains the political systems that rule our
daily lives, and empowers readers to challenge
and change the status quo.

Paperback
November 2017
978 1 5263 6068 7

Trans Mission
by Alex Bertie

I like pugs, doughnuts and tattoos. I sleep
with my socks on. Oh, and I'm transgender.
That's the bit that usually throws people.
Being trans is only one part of who I am,
but it's played a huge role in shaping me.
Over the last six years, I've come out to my
family, changed my name, battled the NHS,
started taking male hormones and have had
top surgery. My quest to a beard is almost
complete. This is my story.

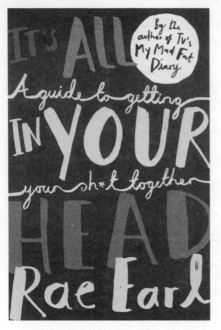

Paperback
August 2017
978 1 5263 0002 7

It's All In Your Head
by Rae Earl

As a teenager, I was very adept at hiding my OCD, my anxiety, my depression and my eating disorders behind a smile and a big sack of silly. And that is why I've written this book. Because I hate to think of any teen going through what I did, and feeling like they need to hide it. This is a book to break down taboos, to start conversations, to help you talk about things that seem impossible. You are not alone.